Miracles Happen Daily

By Antoinette Robinson Dunham

Printed in the United States of America

Published by Natarielle, The Book Doctor

www.natariellethebookdoctor.com

All scriptural references are from the King James Version of the Holy Bible. God and Jesus are referred to in their Hebrew names as Yahweh and Yeshua, respectively.

ISBN- 9798494690906

To the three men who shaped my life:
Edward M. Robinson (my father) who always said a good name is
better than money, and you can be anything you choose to be;
Chester A. Dunham (my Boaz) who loved me into being the woman
God anointed me to be; and
Pastor Freddie Lee Hebron (my spiritual father) who introduced me
to missions and being a conduit for Yahweh's life purpose for me

Miracles Happen Daily

Table of Contents

Foreword 7

Momma, Momma, Look! 9

That's What You Say! 17

One Carat 25

Name Him Stephen 31

ZZZzzzzz 37

You'll Have A Boy Child 47

I'm Saved! I'm Saved! 57

I Need a Black Marker 67

God Says There Is
Healing in the House 75

Granny, I Played in Heaven
with my Sister all Day 83

It's not unto Death 91

Lazarus Arise! 105

Miracles Happen Daily

Foreword

Miracles Happen Daily is a true testament to the greatness of my God. Challenges that presented themselves physically, mentally, or spiritually from childhood into my adulthood were always victorious because of my faith and daily walk with the great I Am. I pray these true-life miracles help strengthen your faith and walk with Yahweh. He is the only true God not made by the hand or the mind of men. Be blessed knowing your father in heaven is aware of your every need. He never sleeps or slumbers where you are concerned.

Miracles Happen Daily

Momma, Momma, Look!

It was a brisk, fall day when my mother pulled our two-toned, brown and beige station wagon into the parking lot of the Chatham County Health Department. There was no joy in my heart. My sisters, Deborah and Edna, and I had dental appointments. Too much Bit-o-Honey candy, I guess. Those were my favorite.

I was afraid I might have a cavity. I hated the dentist probing and pinching my gums. The needle the dentist used to deaden the feeling in my gums was even worse.

Mom led us into the waiting room, telling us to take a seat as she signed our names on the intake sheet at the receptionist's desk. After 90 minutes, we were still waiting to be seen. Mom told us to sit and not move until the dental assistant called our names. She had to run an errand around the block, and she would be right back.

I thought of how hard my father worked. He had two jobs. He left early in the morning and did not return home until late at night. Mom would prepare him two bag lunches: one for each job. Still, our family could not afford a private dentist. Mom said the health department was a blessing to many families, including ours.

Finally, the dental assistant called our names. We followed her into the hall leading to the examination room. She looked at our charts and said, "You all just need cleanings today." "Hurray!" I yelled. She smiled as she sat us into the dental chairs for our cleanings.

After our cleanings, we went outside to wait on our mother. Deborah and Edna sat on a bench in front of the health department, but I started walking along the curve circling the driveway of the health department. There were plenty of leaves, colors so vivid attesting to the fall season: gold, crimson, orange, brown, rust, lime, yellow and cranberry. All blown by the wind, they found their solace nestled against the concave wall of the sidewalk. At ten years of age, I did not realize the earth was proclaiming the great handiwork of the only true, wise God.

I envisioned myself as an acrobat on a tight rope in the circus. I wore silver tights with a beautiful diamond studded bodysuit. My hair was beautifully braided up and twisted with diamond pins sparkling as the spotlight shined on them. A tiara crusted with blue sapphires framed my face.

As I turned around bowing to my audience, I noticed a crumpled, green piece of paper nestled among the leaves. I walked closer. I picked it up, and upon further examination I realized it was a twenty dollar bill. I ran to show it to my sisters and immediately thought of the goodies in the snack machine inside the lobby.

Just then, our mother drove up. I ran to her shouting and waving the twenty dollar bill saying, "Momma! Momma! Look what I found!" Momma smiled and patted me on the head as she placed the folded bill in her purse.

My mother drove straight to the Sunbeam day old bread store. She said each of us could choose one treat. Boy were we glad! Mom bought many loaves of bread and rolls. As she drove, we quietly enjoyed eating our honey buns. We were so happy.

Mom then drove to the M&M Supermarket. We came out of the market with two bags of groceries. As Mom prepared dinner, the smell of fried chicken and cabbage wafted through the house. I was so pleased when we sat down for dinner that evening. My dad really laughed as he enjoyed my mother's delicious meal.

I guess you say, "Where is the Miracle?" Well, the next day, I heard my mother speaking on the phone to her friend. She said, "We did not have much food in the house and no money. Dad was not going to be paid until the end of the week, but God answered my prayers. The miracle of twenty dollars was a gift from heaven. This will carry our family through the week."

I imagined my dad's surprise coming home to that blessed, gifted dinner. For my father in heaven said He would provide our daily bread.

When I look back to my childhood, I can count many times that Abba Father provided all my family's needs. His word shows itself to be true in every part of the lives of His children. When Yeshua shared the Our Father Prayer, He gave us the format of how to pray to His father and opened the door for us.

Meditative Scriptures

Give us this day our daily bread.
Matthew 6:11

Therefore take no thought, saying what shall we eat? What shall we drink? Or, where shall we be clothed?
Matthew 6:31

(For after all these things do the Gentiles seek) For your heavenly father knoweth that ye have need of all these things.
Matthew 6:32

Reflective Thoughts

....

....

....

....

....

....

....

....

....

....

....

Antoinette Robinson Dunham

....

....

....

....

....

....

....

....

....

....

....

....

....

....

Miracles Happen Daily

That's What You Say!

The Robinson household was filled with excitement and joy as we welcomed home our baby brother, Jonas, on December 10th.

Everyone wanted to hold him. Jonas was the youngest of six children, but within weeks of him coming home, our youngest sister, Demetrice, became ill.

My mother noticed Demetrice's inactivity at three years old. She was listless; her body was like a rag doll. She could not hold her head up, and when her arms were lifted and let go, they fell by her sides. Demetrice had a very high fever, and no amount of cold compresses stabilized her temperature.

When our father came home from work and learned of her condition, he took her to be checked. The doctor immediately admitted her to Georgia Infirmary Hospital.

After running tests, the doctor told my father that Demetrice was suffering from bacterial meningitis. He said her chances of survival were slim. The doctor advised our father to make funeral arrangements for Demetrice. My dad said, "That's what you say, but that's not what my God says." I'm quite sure the doctor thought my father was in denial.

When Dad arrived home, he called the doctor so he could explain the diagnosis to our mom. After hanging up the phone, she pulled out her Webster's Dictionary to look up the meaning of bacterial meningitis.

The dictionary read, "Meningitis- An inflammation of the meninges, as the results of infection by bacteria and viruses." My mother immediately started crying, thinking she might lose her youngest daughter. My father still spoke out firmly saying, "Just as I told the doctor, God has the last say. I stand on His words. She will live and not die."

Demetrice was in the hospital a long time. The doctor almost seemed angry with my father because she survived. He acidly said to my father, "She'll never be like other children. She'll never play on a playground, she will be mentally delayed, and she'll never have children." My dad said, "Again I say, that's what you say, but that's not what my God says. She will go home and be treated just like her brothers and sisters."

Fast forward to August of 2021, I asked Demetrice if she remembered anything about her sickness. She said, "I remember being in the hospital, and a man came to my room door. I had my eyes opened but could not move any of my limbs. I could not even lift my head. I could only open my eyes." The man said, "You're such a pretty girl. If you smile for me, I'll give you twenty dollars." Demetrice said, "I don't remember smiling for him, but when I awoke twenty dollars was in a jar on my nightstand. So, I guess I smiled."

Demetrice remembered receiving a small Christmas tree made of gumdrops that sat on her nightstand. She also remembered lying on the sofa with our aunts, Anna and Ossie, and Mom praying for her complete recovery.

Demetrice could not go out and play with us. She talked of laying her head in the windowsill and watching us play. And when we were out of sight, she would imagine us picking blackberries, plums and peaches and playing ball.

When she was old enough to go to school, her medical records followed her, and she was allowed limited activity in gym. When other kids were timed on how fast they ran around the school yard, she could not participate. She felt left out.

Today, Demetrice is a wife, a mother of two and a real estate entrepreneur. By faith, my father and mother stood on God's word. By faith, Demetrice was healed completely, and the Robinson family was blessed.

Meditative Scriptures

But Yeshua beheld their thoughts and said to
them, With men this is impossible, but with
Yahweh all things are possible.
Matthew 19:26

And Yeshua answering saith unto them, Have faith
in Yahweh. For verily I say unto you that
whosoever shall say unto this mountain, Be thou
removed and be thou cast into the sea and shall
not doubt in his heart, but shall believe that those
things which he saith shall come to pass, he shall
have whatsoever he saith.
Mark 11:22-23

Reflective Thoughts

....

....

....

....

....

....

....

....

....

....

....

....

....

....

....

....

....

....

....

....

....

....

....

....

....

....

Miracles Happen Daily

One Carat

I know a lot of women can relate to this phenomenon. I'm not sure about the male gender. Many times, I would look through stores wishing for items hanging on a beautiful mannequin or blinging from the showcase beckoning me to buy. But at that time, I couldn't even afford to buy the gift boxes used to carry these items home.

One Saturday morning, I saw an ad on television for the grand opening of a new jewelry store on Victory Drive. They had all kinds of great deals on diamonds, plus great door prizes. I went thinking maybe I would become a grand prize winner.

I remember browsing through the store; watches, gold bracelets, pearls and diamond earrings glistened out speaking loudly to me saying, "Take me home." My eyes locked onto a beautiful solitaire, one carat diamond ring. I looked down to my hand at the wedding ring I was wearing. It was just a chip that you could barely see, and I longed for an upgrade, hoping that it could be replaced. My husband at that time didn't think buying food was important, much less a diamond ring. It was something I desired in my heart but did not audibly speak about.

I could not afford it. My husband was in college and worked at night. I also worked to help make ends meet. I left the store and did not think about the solitaire diamond again. Fast forward after divorce and many bad relationships, I finally met my Boaz.

My fiancé and I stood in Helzberg's Jewelry to choose our wedding rings. I chose a beautiful gold band. Chester, my fiancé, said, "Why are you choosing such a plain ring?" I responded, "All I want is a band." I felt a band would symbolize my commitment and continuous respect for my husband. He took my arm and steered me across the room to a case of diamond rings saying, "I want you to pick something out for yourself." I kept looking at the prices

and he said, "Pick what you want." He asked the sales clerk
to pull out a couple of solitaire diamond rings. I chose
a half carat ring instead of a one carat because it was what I
liked. Then, the salesclerk brought out two beautiful
baguette diamond wraps to enclose my beautiful diamond
engagement ring. I chose the one that fit perfectly on my
hand.

You would think I would have thought about
the solitaire desire of 26 years before, but it didn't even
cross my mind. One day as I was driving along, the Holy
Spirit reminded me of my desire for the solitaire diamond
ring. I thought about Yahweh's promise to me as His
child. He proved Himself to me *that day* and on many other
occasions.

Meditative Scriptures

Delight yourself also in Yahweh, and He will give
you the desires of your heart.
Psalm 37:4

Commit your way to Yahweh, trust also in Him;
and He shall bring it to pass.
Psalm 37:5

Reflective Thoughts

. . . .

. . . .

. . . .

. . . .

. . . .

. . . .

. . . .

. . . .

. . . .

. . . .

Miracles Happen Daily

....

....

....

....

....

....

....

....

....

....

....

....

....

....

....

Name Him Stephen

I remember my forth pregnancy with mixed emotions. Joy, pain, heartbreak and indecision attacked my mind. It was November of 1982, and my third child, Sareka, was a toddler. This would be my fourth child and my second marriage. My husband still considered playing cards, shooting pool and hanging out with the boys a second job.

I was feeling anxious for days. I was working seventy hours a week in my beauty salon, which did not help my state of mind. I felt overburdened with the responsibilities of wife, mother and salon owner.

After driving Lacy and Jay to school and Sareka to daycare, I returned home to my Monday list of chores. Sunday and Monday were my only days off. I placed clothes in the washer, tidied up the kitchen and made the beds. As I started vacuuming, tears began to flow; I felt hopeless and lost.

I asked myself what was I doing. I was not June Cleaver. It was hard for me to keep the house spotless, and many times I was not able to attend PTA meetings. I was definitely not the Perfect Mom. I felt like Worthless Mom, and here I was having another child.

The tears continued to flow as I found myself sitting in the living room focusing on the beige sofa covered in periwinkle and blue flowers. I felt anguish in my heart, and the question in my mind blared out, *What will you do with another child?* I fell into the New Age Movement. The one that said You can bring home the bacon, fry it in the pan, clean the house, care for the kids, cut the grass, feed the dog (you get the idea) and still please your man. These are lies from the pit of hell.

I screamed out to my heavenly father. What will I do with another child? How will I pay two daycare expenses? I don't know if I even want another child. I don't even know what to name him.

Immediately the Holy Spirit spoke, "Name Him Stephen." I ran to get my Bible. Even though I didn't read it often, I had one. I wanted to know more about this Stephen.

I found out the name Stephen meant "Crowned." In Acts 6:8, it says Stephen was full of faith and power. He did great wonders and signs among the people. I was humbled and grateful that my God, the Great I Am, answered my cry. He let me know He heard my request.

I again cried out to Yahweh saying, "Father I don't want my son stoned." Stephen was chosen to bring peace to the quarreling church. Stephen was mighty in scripture, and he was the first martyr. I know God has named many servant-hearted men in the Bible including His son, Yeshua. I trust His word, and I trusted His wisdom in naming my son.

Meditative Scriptures

And Stephen full of faith and power, did great
wonders and miracles among the people.
Acts 6:8

And all things, whatsoever you shall ask in prayer,
believing, ye shall receive.
Matthew 21:22

Reflective Thoughts

....

....

....

....

....

....

....

....

....

....

....

....

....

....

....

....

....

....

....

....

....

....

....

....

....

ZZZZZZZZZZZZZZZZZ

When a man came into my beauty salon bearing a beautiful, juicy, red apple, I should have thought of Eve accepting the fruit offered to her that took all humanity into darkness.

Instead, my empty and low self-esteem jumped for joy. Edwin came into my life when I was at my lowest point. He was offering compliments and promises of undivided love. He offered what every woman wants: a strong, loving partner to traverse life's ups and downs.

Edwin was my new hair product representative, and he came into my salon with all the charisma of Don Juan. My marriage was shattered. It was full of continuous infidelity. I saw him as my way out to a more stable relationship.

Once we became an item, he treated me like a priceless jewel. I really felt loved. I became pregnant, and we decided to get married. Edwin managed my salon, and eventually we opened two more salons. I was working seven days a week. I noticed Edwin was staying out late, and we began to argue. I started to see signs of an affair. Then the physical abuse began. I would fight back, but it did not deter his mean spirit.

I remember going to church with a black eye. I wore sunglasses through the whole service. One of my mother's old sayings was "Don't jump from the frying pan into the fire." That's exactly what I had done. I was in the fire, and it was hoooooot! She also said a new broom sweeps clean, but eventually it begins to drop straws. I was picking up broom straws constantly. Edwin was losing plenty of straws in the form of constantly losing jobs. He was already working part time managing the salons, and we decided he would manage them fulltime. I felt that working seven days a week would take some of the stress of the business side off of me.

Business was great. I had five employees, and clients were faithful. Money was being made, but Edwin was constantly investing in all sorts of quick, money-making schemes. Not one made a profit.

Early one Tuesday morning, the bank called to tell me I had about 24 bounced checks. In ten years I had never had a bounced check. I went to the bank, and they helped me out by removing the overdraft fees. I know you say this is an awful situation. Just bear with me; there is still more to this story.

I remember getting ready for work because the one constant other than my children were my loyal patrons. My appointments were booked back-to-back. The salon was full. I'd just placed three patrons under the dryer and began roller-setting Mrs. White's hair when the salon door opened and two men in navy suits with badges stepped inside. They asked for me by name. I walked up to them to inquire what they needed.

One of the men said, "We have just left your house, and there is an issue with your gas bill." I asked them to come into the back office so as not to disturb my customers and for privacy.

They further informed me that they had just removed a padlock from my basement door because we were stealing gas. They also said they had a warrant to do it. I was in shock!

The two gentlemen added that I'd been illegally using gas for almost two years. I told them my gas bill had always been paid, maybe not on time, but I always paid my gas bill. My husband was handling all of our bills, and I'd never seen a past due gas bill come to my home.

The officer said, "We have written you constantly to no avail." When he handed me the stack of bills and notices, I realized the mail was being forwarded to a post office box. I had no knowledge that Edwin had forwarded the mail.

The amount of service stolen came to thousands of dollars. The action was a felony charge. I did not want to go to jail. I had a shop full of clients. My mind was swirling. I prayed, *Father, what can I do?*

I knew one of the officers, but he did not say much at first. He was my high school classmate. He knew me personally. He turned to the other officer and said, "I know Antoinette very well. She's always been a business owner and a lawful citizen. I believe she had no idea what her husband was doing."

The gentlemen talked among themselves, while looking over the statements. They decided to reduce my balance, and I would have three months to pay the reduced amount.

The old saying, "When it rains, it pours," was definitely true for me. The next day I received a registered letter. After signing for it, I hurried into the house to read it.

The letter informed me that my house was in foreclosure. My mortgage note had not been paid in nine months. Mercy Yeshua! I cried out as I sat on the front staircase of my 1900 Victorian dream home with its mantles in every room. I looked over at the stained glass window on top of the front door.

I thought of all the money I invested into this house and four other properties. I worked seven days a week thinking I was a part of a team; instead I was sleeping with a demonic enemy. My mate was the enemy of my soul.

Where would my children and I live? I could not take anymore. I felt so dejected, used and abused. Suddenly, I heard a loud noise. I looked around. Where was it coming from? It sounded like a gigantic swarm of locusts.

ZZZZZZZZZZZZZZZZZZZZZZ,ZZZZZZZZ
ZZZZZZZ,ZZZZZZZZZZZZZ, ZZZZZZZZZZZZZ
ZZZZZZZZZZZZZZZZZZZZZZZZZZZZZZZZZ
Z. Oh God, the sound was deafening and it was coming

from inside of my head. I spoke out loudly saying,

"Father, if this is a nervous breakdown, I don't have time

for it. I have my children to care for!" Immediately, the

noise stopped.

This was another life-altering situation that almost sent

me to Georgia Regional Mental Facility. Yet, my God, He

kept my mind, when the onslaught of the enemy sought to

take me from my children, to take my very life. The

compassion of the only true and wise God with His

amazing grace redeemed me. I cried out, and He answered

me in my distress. The tumultuous and abusive situation I

put myself in was because I ran to a male and not to the

living God. Only He could heal the wounds deep inside of

me.

I walked away from my house, but God kept my mind.

He kept me from losing my precious children and the

business I'd worked so hard to build. The house is a

material thing that can always be replaced, but the

devastation of a mental breakdown would have had several

lasting effects. I'm so grateful to Yahweh that he granted me a miracle and kept my mind!

Meditative Scriptures

Surely He shall deliver thee from snares of the fowler and from the noisome pestilence. He shall cover thee with His feathers and under His wings shall thou trust. His truth shall be thy shield and buckler.
Psalm 91:3-4

But know that Yahweh has set apart him that is godly for himself: Yaheweh will hear when I call upon Him.
Psalm 4:3

Reflective Thoughts

....

....

....

....

....

....

....

....

....

....

....

Miracles Happen Daily

....

....

....

....

....

....

....

....

....

....

....

....

....

....

You'll Have a Boy Child

Looking back to the weekend, when my husband, Allen, did not come home, I was worried, wondering where he could be. Friday and Saturday I continually called his cell phone; he never answered.

I decided to get up early Sunday morning and search the city of Savannah. My seven year old and I went riding up and down the streets of Chatham County. I was playing a game of "That's my Car" with EJ while I was looking for a particular van.

About forty minutes into my search, EJ hollered "Momma! Momma, look there's our van!" There glistening in the morning sun was our burgundy van parked in front of a seedy motel.

I parked and went inside of the motel office. There was a man at the front desk, and I said, "Good morning, can you tell me if you have a Coster registered in room 22?" He nastily said, "I don't have anything to do with this." He then turned and walked away from the desk into his office.

His wife was standing at the desk looking on. She looked me in the eyes; her eyes were filled with empathy and compassion. I knew she had seen many wives come searching for wayward husbands. She said, "I'm tired of this mess," and handed me the keys. I looked in my hands and saw the number 22 on the tag. I thanked her, and she bowed in respect of one wife to another. I could feel her pain.

As I put the keys into the door and pushed it open, a woman inside ran and tried to close the door. She said, "If he wanted you to know where he was, he would have told you." I shoved past her and saw my husband run into the bathroom closing the door. I pushed on the bathroom door, but he held fast, not wanting to confront me face-to-face.

I turned my attention to look at the female that kept Allen's attention this weekend. She had on black hot pants, a black sweater and black army boots with a black cap turned backwards on her head.

Her face showed signs of a hard life. Her lips were discolored from years of drugging, her skin dulled and eyes empty. What did Allen have in common with this woman? The pipe on the dresser told a story along with an aluminum soda can and pieces of crack cocaine. On the floor sat several brown paper bags.

I worked many hours in my beauty salon. Several customers would make disconcerting remarks.

"I saw young boys driving your car today Downtown."

"Not my car," I said. "There are plenty of tan Toyota Camrys. They all look alike."

I was in deep denial. Ms. Hattie also mentioned seeing a group of young men in my car riding on Henry Street one evening as she left the salon. Signs were everywhere. Missing money, lost jobs, late hours, secret conversations in his man cave and many unfamiliar acquaintances.

I left the motel angry and hurt. I wanted a divorce There would be no lasting attachments because we did not have any children together. That was one blessing I could be thankful for.

Early on Monday morning my friend Phyllis and I went to the Westly Health Department. She came for moral support. I wanted to have every test known to man for sexually transmitted diseases.

The nurse took many different vials of blood. Then she gave me a cup to give her a urine sample. I asked her why she needed a urine sample. She let me know it was for a pregnancy test. I said, "I don't need a pregnancy test; I only came for sexually transmitted disease tests." She let me know the pregnancy test was one of the listed choices used to complete this slate of test. If I did not give her a urine specimen, I could not receive any of the test results. I took a deep breath and went into the bathroom and provided the urine sample, placing it on the allotted tray on the two way window inside.

We waited in the waiting room for about two hours talking about my situation, among other things. Finally, the nurse came to speak to me. She informed me that all but one of my results came back negative. I looked up puzzled. She laughed saying, "Your AIDS test has to be sent off, and you will go talk to the health counselor before you leave. She will explain that process to you. I sighed a great breath of relief.

Then she said, "Mrs. Coster there's one more thing; I don't know if this is good news or bad news, but you're pregnant." I cried out in shock and disbelief. The tears would not stop, I did not want to be forever attached to Allen.

Phyllis and the nurse tried to console me but were unsuccessful. Just then the counselor called my name. I walked into her office in a daze. She introduced herself and placed a sheet of paper on the desk, letting me know that in one week I could call the number provided on the sheet and once the voice activated machine picked up, I would put in the code number she gave me. The machine would reply negative or positive according to my test results. *Another week in turmoil.*

I raised up out of my seat to leave, but the counselor placed her hand on top of my hand, and I sat back in my chair. She said,"God has given me a word for you. He said do not leave your husband. You are going to have a rough pregnancy. You will have a boy child, and he will be a blessing to you." I thanked her as I walked out of her office, still in disbelief.

I did not leave Allen, and my pregnancy certainly was difficult. At five months of pregnancy, I had to stop working. Close to my delivery time, I went into the hospital every other day for an ultrasound test.

On June 25th, I was admitted into the hospital with labor pains, and leaking amniotic fluid. All through the night I was in excruciating pain. Early the next morning, Dr. Persad came into my room.

"Good morning Ms. Antoinette, I want to let you know we must perform a C-Section on you today. Your membrane ruptured last night, and I was not informed. You have no fluids left, and we cannot do a dry delivery."

He turned to the nurses, angrily ordering them to prepare me, and take me to the operating room immediately. As I was rolled toward the room, I prayed. *Father, please continue to keep your hands upon me.* This was my sixth delivery and my first C-section.

As the perioperative nurse placed the nasal cannula in my nose, the other placed my legs in the stirrups and pulled a sheet over the lower part of my body.

I could hear Dr. Persad talking to the nurses. Suddenly, I felt a marked line being drawn across my lower abdomen, and I yelled out, "Dr. Persad, are you going to give me some pain meds?" He replied, Ms. Antoinette, you have not been given anesthesia?"

"No, sir." He threw some profane language around as he asked, "Where is the anesthesiologist?"

I thought to myself, it's just like that tricky demon, Satan, to try to kill me on the operating table and foil God's prophecy concerning my son.

The anesthesiologist found his place in the room putting a needle full of meds into my IV, which took me to the land of sweet sleep.

I went on to deliver a healthy, baby boy. The prophecy was given when I was only two weeks pregnant. No test at that time could accurately give the gender of a child. I had no symptoms. Yahweh Himself gave me this child, and He Himself made him my blessing.

Meditative Scriptures

Adonai (The Lord) bless you and
keep you. Adonai maketh His face shine upon you
and be gracious to you. Adonai lifts up His
countenance upon you and give you peace.
Numbers 6:24-26 (ESV)

Before I created you in the womb, I knew you.
Before you were born, I set you apart. I made you
a prophet to the nations.
Jeremiah 1:5

Reflective Thoughts

....
....
....
....
....
....
....
....
....
....
....

Miracles Happen Daily

....

....

....

....

....

....

....

....

....

....

....

....

....

I'm Saved! I'm Saved!

The day of December 14, 1999 changed my life forever. I received a disturbing phone call informing me that my brother, Ed, had been stabbed or shot in his home. When I got this call, I was told that my father was inside of Ed's house with the police. I could not imagine the pain and agony my father felt, watching his namesake possibly lying lifeless on the floor. No one else was allowed inside.

I did not know for sure if my brother was dead or alive. I had just started perming three young sisters' hair. Sareka, their mom, dropped them off and would pick them up once their perms were completed. I had to finish their hair service. I had to do my job.

When I reached my brother's house three hours later, family and friends were outside on the lawn waiting for news of Ed's condition. Yellow and black crime tape corded off the porch keeping us away.

When the paramedics rolled out my brother's lifeless body covered on the gurney, a chorus of screams mingled with wounded moans filled the air like a heavy blanket. My brother was dead at 39 years old.

My siblings, myself and our dad returned home to the house we all grew up in, asking ourselves who or why would anyone take Ed's life, killing him in his own home. We knew that an even harder task lay ahead of our family.

Our mother was out of town taking part in a senior's Christmas excursion to Maggio's Farm. The bus full of seniors left at noon, all seats occupied with laughing and singing as the bus pulled from the center's parking lot. My daughter, Salathia, and Tonya (my brother's girlfriend) rode along with me, to pick our mother up from the center. The bus was scheduled to arrive at 9:00 pm. As Mom retreated from the bus, I was on pins and needles, trying to act natural. Mom walked toward my car smiling. After exchanging pleasantrics, we headed home.

Mom was very talkative, sharing how beautifully the farm was decorated. She said every roof, tree, building and fence was lit with Christmas lights, and the mangers were breathtaking.

Mom was so joyful. As I drove home, I held back my tears, not wanting to alarm her in any way. I was thankful that Salathia and Tonya were there to keep the conversation moving.

When my car turned onto our street, Mom asked, "Why are all those cars at the house? What has happened?" I said, "Mom, please come into the house. Dad has something to share with you."

As we entered the living room, my father put his arms around my mother and said, "Lo, I hate to tell you this, but Ed was shot today, and he's dead. He's gone."

My mom moaned loudly with the deep guttural sound of a wounded, helpless soul in pain. Mom screamed out, "I was so happy; the day was too perfect. You can never be too happy. Horrible things happen."

She sobbed crumbling to the floor. Family members tried to pick her up from the floor, but my sister,

Demetrice, hollered, "Let her go; let her stay there." My mother had to be sedated and put to bed.

Ed was loving and full of life. He respected older neighbors, and he loved children. He was on the football team at Savannah High School and received a full scholarship to Virginia State. He had a high IQ and was an outstanding student. He longed for home, not graduating from college. He moved back to Savannah where he was accepted into the police academy and served many years in law enforcement. Our family was so proud of his accomplishments.

Everything seem to be going well for Ed, but the unseen, evil forces infiltrated Ed's life through the crack pipe. Ed's girlfriend, Kila, was hooked on the pipe. Ed told her, "You have to stop smoking that stuff. You can get me fired from my job." He decided to take a pull to show her how easy it was for her to stop smoking. The puff he took from Satan's pipe pulled my brother down to his pit of a living hell. This demonically invented drug cause countless people to fall. My brother was no exception.

My sister, Deborah, spear-headed the arrangements for Ed's funeral. We did not want our parents to suffer anymore by going through the heartbreak of planning Ed's funeral.

Looking back to the day we laid my brother to rest, I remember walking into St. Benedict The Moor Catholic Church, surrounded by family and friends, yet I felt all alone. I remember walking in a fog-like cloud. I saw everything going on around me, but it was as if I was looking on, not taking part in the service.

My mind kept wondering *did my brother make it into God's kingdom? Did he choose Yahweh?* I did not mention my concerns to anyone, not even my husband, Chester.

When the service was over and we went to the cemetery for Ed's interment, I was surprised to see two miniature Christmas trees. The spruce had red velvet bows and the pine had gold bells. When they finished covering Ed's casket, the pine lay at his head and the spruce at the bottom of Ed's grave.

My mom said, "Merry Christmas, son! You will miss Christmas this year!" We left the gravesite and went home to love on each other. We also celebrated my son, EJ's, 11th birthday that day. He said this was the saddest birthday he'd ever celebrated.

Two months after Ed's funeral, as I was getting ready for bed, I noticed a decorated bottle of wine that was on my dresser for years was empty. I laughed; nobody but Ed. I left him at my house earlier in December manicuring my lawn. I laughed to myself as I lied down to sleep, saying aloud, "That's my brother."

I awoke the next morning to the sound of bells ringing. I opened my eyes and blinked. In front of me was a miniature pine branch with gold bells being shook in my face. Ching Ring, Ring, Ring, Ring, Ching. I heard my brother's voice saying, "I'm saved, I'm saved! Thank God, I'm saved. No more chains binding me, I'm saved!"

From the very moment I heard my brother's voice, I knew my heavenly father, the great I Am, heard my inner cry. He felt my pain and agony in the lost of my dear brother. He did not forsake my brother when the enemy of Ed's soul tried to destroy him through drugs. My father said No! He belongs to me. Yahweh's grace was sufficient in Ed's life.

What Satan meant for harm and destruction, grace recovered. Hallelujah!!!!!

Meditative Scriptures

And He saved them from the hand of him that
hated them and redeemed them from the hand of
the enemy.
Psalm 106:10

I call the heavens and the earth to witness about
you today, that I have set before you life and death,
the blessing and the curses: therefore choose life in
order that you and your descendants may live.
Deuteronomy 30:19 (AMP)

Reflective Thoughts

....

....

....

....

....

....

....

....

....

....

....

....

Antoinette Robinson Dunham

....

....

....

....

....

....

....

....

....

....

....

....

....

....

Miracles Happen Daily

I Need a Black Marker

Going to Haiti has always blessed me. Mission work has given me a servant's heart. April 2010 was especially taxing for me. It was three months after the 7.0 earthquake rocked Haiti. As we embarked from the airplane, I wondered what we would encounter in Haiti.

The world news said two hundred thousand people were killed in the earthquake. I wanted to see Haiti for myself. I wanted to be there for our Christian Revival and Restoration Center (CRRC) staff and family. As we drove from Toussaint Louverture International Airport, the billboards along the street spoke of a happier time.

I could not believe what I was seeing: small tents nestled on every empty piece of land, even parks and playgrounds. To see the horrific conditions firsthand ripped my heart wide open. Children were playing on giant mounds of collapsed buildings. Kids just enjoying being kids, running in the rubble, digging ditches and drawing in the dirt.

We in America could not imagine our children in such chaos. Even before the earthquake, trash, contaminated water and poor living conditions were harsh. Now they were even harsher.

Riding along, my eyes caught sight of a band of boys. Five young men between the ages of twelve and fourteen were walking along the side of the road. They were laughing and joking. One of the mates' left leg was amputated up to his thigh, yet he kept up the pace with the aid of a long stick. It was so painful to look upon, much more painful for one so young to endure.

When we arrived at our temporary mission house (CRRC's mission house was destroyed in the earthquake), Pastor Freddie greeted our team, and we started unloading our supplies. There were tents all around the building within the fenced yard. Mothers were preparing meals and washing clothes, hanging them on tree limbs and fences. Children were running around the yard playing; babies were crying. Need cried out everywhere.

The next morning, Pastor Kim suggested we go to CRRC's warehouse to retrieve clothing, shoes, hygiene products, food, water and anything pertaining to infants.

The team loaded into our van followed by a pickup truck headed to the storage unit. The ride would take twice as long because of the terrible road conditions. We saw even more damage caused by a few minutes of the earth-shifting out of place.

Once we arrived at the storage yard, we saw many of the cement block units broken, doors opened, and roofs caved in. We could see the once-protected merchandise now unguarded, free for the taking.

When we pulled our vehicles up to CRRC's unit, we saw no damage whatsoever. Praise Jehovah! As we entered the three thousand square foot building, Pastor Kim gave instructions. She said, "Let's set up boxes against the empty wall opposite the stored merchandise. We will be pulling clothing, shoes, hygiene products and food." She emphasized gathering everything we saw useable for infants and small children.

The wall where the brown cardboard boxes sat, waiting to be filled with critically needed items, was 30 feet away from the filled shelves and bins that lined the unit's wall. We had eight brothers and sisters in Christ going from the container to the boxes with the required goods. We soon discovered infant's clothing mixed in with the men's clothing, boy's clothing mixed in with girl's clothing, and shoes mixed in all boxes. You get the drift: we had not marked the boxes. "Does anyone have a black, permanent marker," I asked. Everyone checked in their backpacks. We ended up with one pencil and a blue, fine point pen. Try using those on brown cardboard boxes to label them. We could barely see the print. I silently spoke to myself saying "Lord, we need a black, permanent marker."

To my amazement, in the second box I opened after my silent plea, I found one black, Bic permanent marker. The box was filled with assorted clothing and belts, but it had a black, permanent marker, just one. I could not believe it: not a pack, or a box with school supplies, but just what I asked for, just what we needed. Jehovah Jireh, my provider! Praise Him!

He really does read our minds. He knows everything we have need of, and He does have a sense of humor. We marked each cardboard box with large blocked print, which made our task easier to complete.

Meditative Scriptures

Before they call, I will answer; while yet they
are yet speaking I will hear.
Isaiah 65: 24

And this is the confidence that we have in him,
that if we ask anything according to his will, He
heareth us. And if we know that He heareth us,
whatsoever we ask, we know that we have the
petitions that we desired of Him.
1 John 5:14-15

Reflective Thoughts

....

....

....

....

....

....

....

....

....

....

....

Miracles Happen Daily

....

....

....

....

....

....

....

....

....

....

....

....

....

....

God Says There Is
Healing in the House

One Sunday, I decided to accept an invitation from my adopted daughter, Donna, to go workout with her at the gym on Hunter Army Base. We decided to meet every Monday at 10 a.m.. Donna was in great shape. She was Army ready, unlike me. For over two years, a back injury caused me to acquire a sedentary lifestyle. I was now ready to get physical. I was ready to shed some extra, unwanted pounds. I was done with moving my buttons on my pants.

Donna's encouragement would help kickstart my desire to become fit. Once we arrived on base, we walked outside for thirty minutes to warm up. Then, we went inside to the well-equipped gym.

I followed Donna, imitating everything she did. We went from the arm press to the leg lift; next was the inner thigh press, then we moved on to ride the stationary bike. Donna said, "Let's work on our upper arms." We did three sets of twenty on the dumbbells followed by a cool down on the treadmill. We congratulated each other for our well-coordinated workout.

I felt energized. We planned to meet next week: same time, same place. Well, three days later I received an unwelcomed surprise: I could not lift my right arm. The pain brought me to tears. I could not bathe or brush my teeth. Even when I breathed, it hurt. I had to use my left hand and put my right arm in a sling. This pain changed my life, and the pain medicine only made me sleep.

The following Sunday, as I started my car to go to church with my left hand, pain radiated down my right arm. I went into the choir stand feeling inadequate. The choir sings to glorify and praise Yahweh, withholding nothing.

Our choir usually sang six songs on Sunday. After four songs, I was weary and in pain. I could not even clap my hands because of the pain.

I remember saying to myself, *How am I going to go to Haiti next week on our mission trip when I can't raise my arms because of the pain? I won't be able to pull my luggage through the airport!* We were going to Haiti for our pastoral conference. I did not want anything to affect my ability to perform my duties once we arrived in Haiti.

It was not ten minutes later, when I heard Pastor Freddie praying. He said, "God says there's healing in the house." I heard him, but I guess my painful condition caused me not to receive the words Pastor was speaking. Service ended, my grandson, Ethan, and I left church, and I drove home. I cooked dinner, washed dishes and cleaned the counters in the kitchen.

My husband, Chester, was watching television, and I told him I was going to bed. I showered and got into bed. When I laid my head on the pillow the Holy Spirit said, *You have had no pain since you left church.* I remembered: I got in the car, opened the door and turned the key in the ignition with my right hand. I prepared dinner. I bathed and got into bed without any pain whatsoever. I had been completely healed when Pastor Freddie spoke the word.

I could not wait to give my testimony. Yes, my Father heard my plea. My Savior felt my pain. There is healing in the house of Yahweh. Yeshua taught us how to pray. He taught us how to have faith and receive from his Father. So many times in the Bible, Yeshua healed, casted out demons, and set souls free.

He loves his people so much that He gives, and He pays attention to our every need. I know, without a shadow of a doubt, that Sunday's healing word was for me. Even when we do not acknowledge His blessings, He continues to bless, He continues to comfort, and He continues to love us.

Meditative Scriptures

Have mercy upon me, O Yahweh; for I am weak.
O Yahweh, heal me; for my bones are vexed.
Psalm 6:2

I have seen his ways and I will heal him: I will lead
him also and restore comforts unto him and to his
mourners. I create the fruit of the lips. Peace, peace
to him that is far off and to him that is near, saith
the Lord, and I will heal him.
Isaiah 57: 18-19

Reflective Thoughts

....

....

....

....

....

....

....

....

....

....

Antoinette Robinson Dunham

....

....

....

....

....

....

....

....

....

....

....

....

....

....

....

Miracles Happen Daily

Granny, I Played in Heaven with my Sister all Day

It was the fall of the year 2011, and my granddaughter, Kaitlin (who was five years old at the time), spent the night with me. I got up early to cook breakfast for our family. As I was flipping over my last pancake, Kaitlin ran into the kitchen excitedly exclaiming, "Granny, Granny guess what? I was with my sister playing in heaven all day!"

Kaitlin is a surviving twin. Her sister, Kailee, transitioned in 2006 after surgery to reconnect her intestine.

I was worried about little baby Kailee. After her surgery, the doctors said her intestine would have to heal before she could leave the hospital. She was so swollen. My daughter and I were devastated about her condition. Only a few weeks later, the doctors said she was braindead, and there were no signs of her intestine healing. When they gave her milk, it escaped into her body.

My daughter along with the twins' father had a conference with Kailee's doctors. The doctors said they would transition her to Hospice. They would not feed her any nourishment, allowing her to gracefully slip away. I was hopeful. I kept saying give her a couple of weeks, but the doctors kept saying there was no chance of Kailee surviving.

Kailee's parents along with family members visited her constantly in Savannah's Hospice Home. Kailee was the first infant to transition at Hospice in Savannah.

I would wake up at night 12:30 a.m. and get in my car and drive to the Hospice Center to sit with my granddaughter. I did not want her to be alone in the midnight hours. I would sing songs to her. Her favorite was "This Little Light of Mine, I'm Gonna Let it Shine." She would lovingly look at me, trying to mouth the song along with me. I would also recite nursery rhymes to her. I held on believing that my God, the God of Israel, would still perform a miracle in her circumstances.

I knew she was not braindead. Before she left the hospital, she would react to sounds. On the day of her transition, Salathia brought Kaitlin to the community center to take pictures with her sister. When Kaitlin cried out Kailee started looking around for her. Braindead: NO. Unbelief in God's ability: YES. She knew her sister's voice.

I think back to the wonderful day when my heavenly father allowed me to share in Kaitlin's wonderful journey in the spirit. Kaitlin visited her sister and played all around heaven all day long in the presence of El Shaddai, the All-Sufficient One, the God of Israel.

Kaitlin is now 14 years old and does not remember her visit to heaven, but God does. He eased my mind and heart, letting me know that He has my granddaughter playing around heaven. God allowed Kaitlin to join Kailee in His wonderful presence, in His heavenly kingdom. Kaitlin said that after playing all day around heaven, she told her sister she had to leave, but she would see her later.

I think of my own miscarriage, and also my abortion, which I was so ashamed about. I think how self-righteous men define your relationship with God based on their need to control and dominate your destiny and your identity, just like the Sadducees and Pharisees of Jesus's time. These groups judged everyone as if they were sinless, as if they spoke for God instead of their self-righteous selves.

The true God of creation has an eternal place for all His children: those born, living a full life; those who die at a young age; and those aborted because of man's deception in this sinful world.

I know my children and grandchild are enjoying the eternal home that Yeshua spoke of provided by His father in eternity. I know that my God is forgiving. His grace is sufficient, and His love eternal.

Meditative Scriptures

See that you do not despise one of these little ones,
for I tell you that in heaven their angels always see
the face of my Father who is in heaven.
Matthew 18:10

And Peter said to them, "Repent and be
baptized every one of you in the name of Yeshua
Messiah for the forgiveness of your sins, and you
will receive the gift of the Holy Spirit. For the
promise is for you and for your children and for all
who are far off, everyone whom the Lord Our
God calls to Himself.
Acts 2: 38-39

So it is not the will of my Father who is in heaven
that one of these little ones should perish.
Matthew: 18-14

Reflective Thoughts

....

....

....

....

....

....

....

....

....

....

....

Antoinette Robinson Dunham

....

....

....

....

....

....

....

....

....

....

....

....

....

Miracles Happen Daily

It's Not Unto Death

On March 2, 2014, I awoke to the ringing of my phone. It was 7:05 a.m.. Looking at the caller ID, I realized it was my husband, Chester.

"Hello Honey," I answered.

He replied singing, "Get out in that kitchen and rattle those pots and pans. I say Get out in that kitchen and rattle those pots and pans. This is your wakeup call."

I laughed, "Thank you honey for calling me. Are you going to Church today?" "I don't know. It depends on how I feel when I leave work."

"OK Honey, I will see you later." I joyfully replied.

He laughed saying, "Later."

I jumped out of bed and went downstairs to wake Ethan and Kiah (our grands). I placed their clothes on the chair and directed them to wash their faces and brush their teeth. "No horsing around! Get dressed; we have to get to church on time." This was my Sunday to prepare breakfast for our Sunday School. I already had the salmon croquettes cooked and eggs and grits packed up to transport.

The phone suddenly rang again. I picked it up thinking Chester was calling back. "Hello Honey," I answered. The voice on the other line was not Chester's. "Hello Mrs. Dunham. This is Harris; I'm working with Chester. There's been an accident on the ship, and he's been injured. He's laying down, and we're waiting with him. There is an ambulance on the way. Chester informed the dispatcher that he wanted to be transported to St. Joseph's Hospital because it is closer to your home."

"Thank you. I will meet you there," I said. It was about 7:15 when I hung up the phone. I could not imagine what could have happened so quickly. I ran upstairs to tell my sister-in-law, Janie, who was visiting from California, about the accident.

After relaying the conversation Harris and I had about Chester's accident to Janie, suddenly my spirit started shouting Hallelujah for about sixty seconds. Repeatedly, I cried out in praise to my heavenly father. I believe at that time Yahweh let me know He was still in control.
We hurriedly dressed, and I asked Antonio, our youngest son, to take Ethan, Kiah and the prepared breakfast to the church. I also asked him to let Ms. Anne know about the accident. Thank God, Antonio had recently become a licensed driver.

As Janie and I drove speedily down Hwy 204 to St. Joseph's, my mind raced with questions. Why would Chester be on the ship? He usually sent crews to work on the ship. He was a Header at ILA 1414. Why was he in an accident on the ship?

The ambulance that transported Chester was still idling in the driveway at the emergency room door. I rushed to the intake desk explaining to the nurse that my husband was injured on the job and was transported from Georgia Ports to St. Joseph. She said, "Yes, he's just been brought in. We're assessing his condition and taking his vital signs. But he seems fine. Just have a seat and a nurse will come to talk to you soon." Just her saying he seems fine helped me feel better about the situation.

Forty-five minutes later we were taken into Chester's room. He was hooked up to all sorts of monitors and IVs. He had an aspen collar around his neck. The nurse asked if he had diabetes because he'd lost consciousness temporarily. She said the aspen collar was in place because they suspected neck and brain trauma. When I spoke to Chester, he said "I don't understand what happened. The road was straight, and then it raised up." The nurse said we had to leave because he was being transported for a c-scan.

They would let us know the extent of his injuries afterwards. I looked at my husband. He had a large bruise on his forehead. I told Chester I would be waiting when he returned from his c-scan. Janie said, "See you later Chest," and we walked back into the waiting room.

Janie and I decided to go to Waffle House for coffee and breakfast. We'd just began to place our order when I suddenly felt a queasiness in the pit of my stomach. Immediately my phone rang. I answered saying hello. "Hello Mrs. Dunham, this is Debbie from St. Joseph's. We're concern about what we see on Mr. Dunham's catscan, and we're transporting him to Memorial Health

University where the trauma team will take over. The neurology surgeon, Dr. Thompson, will continue his care. The injuries Mr. Dunham has will better be addressed by a trauma team. You don't have to rush. It will take us an hour or more to transport him." As I hung up the phone, Janie informed me that she had already cancelled our breakfast order.

We decided to pick up coffee and muffins from Starbucks on our way to Memorial. We arrived at noon. I inquired at the desk about Chester, and the receptionist said he had not been admitted to the hospital yet.

Meanwhile family and friends began to arrive. People kept asking questions we could not answer. One of Chester's co-workers said Chester was driving his truck on a RORO ship and had an accident. After inquiring at the intake desk for the fourth time, I learned that Chester was admitted hours ago, but under the name John Doe. The explanation was that he was transported by ambulance, and his name had never been placed into the database.

Three hours later, I walked into an operating room transformed into an emergency intake room for Chester. The halls were lined with cots containing sick people waiting to be admitted into the hospital. I approached

Chester's bed noticing he was conscious, but his face grimaced with pain. He had a large bandage across his forehead and dried blood on his hands. He tried to talk, but he seemed to be in a daze. He kept repeating, "I don't understand; the road was straight."

Only two family members were allowed in his room at a time. We kept visits to ten-minute intervals. The emergency room nurses came in constantly monitoring his vital signs. The emergency room doctor came into the room and introduced himself. The doctor said Chester had not been medicated at that time because they wanted him to stay lucid.

We stayed in the operating/intake room until 2:30 a.m. Monday morning. By this time, it was only Chester and me. I prayed constantly wondering what would happen to my Boaz. That was my nickname for Chester. Finally, the nurse came to wheel Chester up to PCU. She allowed me to ride up in the elevator with him. The nurse directed me to wait in the family waiting room, and she would call me when Chester was comfortable in his room.

When I went into Chester's room, he was asleep. I settled down in the big comfortable recliner and tried to sleep; it had been a long day. Nurses came in all through the night. I asked one nurse why the room was completely white: bed, walls, ceiling and floors. There was no color anywhere in Chester's room. He said there are only bright and colorful cartoon characters and forest scenes in pediatrics.

The next morning Chester's condition worsened. I would even say the injuries began to show themselves, and Chester was in deep, physical trouble. He was highly agitated and kept asking why he couldn't go home.

Later that night a male nurse came into the room. After charting Chester's vitals, he noticed Chester's rapid breathing and twisting in bed. He coughed, and the nurse thought he might be congested with mucus. The nurse placed a suctioning tube down Chester's throat and cut on the machine. I could hear the whooshing sound of the machine as it pulled mucus, but after several hours there was very little being drawn out. Chester, being the independent man he is, snatched the tube saying, "I'll do it myself." The nurse took the tube back from him and began suctioning again. Suddenly, bright red blood began to flow into the tube. I said "Enough! As long as you have been suctioning, there is very little mucus, and now bright red blood is coming out of Chester's throat. Evidently mucus is not the problem."

He then asked, "Does your husband have sleep apnea?" I said, "Past testing said no." The nurse said Chester's breathing sounded like he did have sleep apnea. The nurse left the room and came back with an oxygen tank. When he put the nasal cannula in Chester's nose, his body immediately relaxed a little, but not completely. The nurse went out and came back with a larger oxygen tank and hooked it up. Instantly, the increased airflow caused Chester's body to completely relax.

The next morning, Dr. Thompson came into Chester's room and introduced himself. He placed x-rays on a screen and explained that Chester's neck was broken in three places, and he might have a concussion. Dr. Thompson moved Chester to the ICU. Chester was sedated and surgery would be performed the next morning.

I went home to bathe and rest. I woke up the next morning and asked Yahweh to be with Chester. Five o' clock a.m., I opened my front door and walked onto the porch. There perched above my neighbor's roof was the biggest, brightest star; it reminded me of the star used to direct the wise men to the young child, Jesus. Yahweh was letting me know He was still with us.

Family and friends gathered in the lobby to sit with me as we waited for Dr. Thompson and his team to repair Chester's broken neck. Dr. Thompson previously remarked that Chester had the same injuries as Christopher Reeve. He said Chester's injuries could have left him paralyzed. He also remarked that Chester was lucky.

I know it was not luck. When Chester's condition was critical and his breathing erratic, I went into the bathroom to pray. I asked Yahweh was Chester going to live. I heard the words, "Not unto Death." Those are the same words Bev prophesied a month before the accident.

I called Bev the next morning asking her to convey her dream to me. She said, "You were standing in a room by a bed. A person was lying in the bed covered with a white sheet. I could not see who the person was. The walls, floor and ceiling were all white in color, and God said to tell you it was Not unto Death." My God was prophesying this event before it even happened.

As family and friends sat in the hospital lobby's waiting area with me during the many hours it took for Dr. Thompson and his team to perform the surgery, I felt comfort and assurance Yeshua was with us. Pastor Tillman, Chester's pastor, continually prayed and stayed with us until the surgery was completed.

Dr. Thompson came out to us smiling saying the surgery went well, but when he opened Chester's neck he was surprised by a bruised area inside that had clotted. Now I knew where the blood was coming from in the suction tube. The clot could have moved, but I know our God is always on time.

Later that night, I received a call from Dr. Thompson; he had bad news. He said after going over the after-surgery x-rays, he saw where the screw between the 1st and 2nd vertebrae was too long, and if Chester just turned his neck the wrong way the point of the screw would lacerate his spinal cord.

Chester had to go back to surgery early the next morning. Again, we sat in the lobby waiting for news. When Dr. Thompson came out, he was flashing his million-dollar smile saying, "All is well." He said "I could not sleep last night, thinking about that screw and what damage it would do if Chester just turned his neck the wrong way." We cheered and hugged each other and gave praise to the True and Living God.

After many months of therapy, Chester made a full recovery, and I know who appointed and anointed Chester's complete healing.

Meditative Scriptures

He shall call upon me, and I will answer him: I will
be with him in trouble; I will deliver him and
honor him.
Psalm 91:15

With long life will I satisfy him and show him my
salvation.
Psalm 91:16

Reflective Thoughts

....

....

....

....

....

....

....

....

....

....

....

Miracles Happen Daily

. . . .

. . . .

. . . .

. . . .

. . . .

. . . .

. . . .

. . . .

. . . .

. . . .

. . . .

. . . .

. . . .

. . . .

Lazarus Arise!

March 21, 2015 started out as a beautiful spring day with butterflies fluttering, competing with bumblebees for residence on lilac, ficus, hibiscus and beautiful, gold sunflowers. The air permeated with the luscious smell of white, honeysuckle flowers nearby.

My sister, Deborah, and I were just beginning to tour a beautiful home on our list from the annual Savannah Tour of Homes fundraiser. I worked all week as a docent and looked forward to touring the beautiful homes that were this year's pick for outstanding residences.

We were talking with Linda, one of the planners for the tour. Suddenly, Deborah's pager went off. She grabbed my arm, pulling me away in mid sentence. It startled me, and I gave her the look of *how rude*. She said Dad's emergency alert necklace went off. She'd received a text saying he was in distress.

My sister ran every red light with her emergency lights flashing, and when we turned onto the street we grew up on, the red and white ambulance was sitting in front of our house. I jumped out of the car and stepped up on the running board to peek in at my dad.

The paramedic was pressing on Dad's chest and suddenly a large piece of meat flew out of his mouth onto the floor. He then checked for clarity and placed an oxygen mask on Dad's mouth. The gentleman let us know they were on their way to Candler Hospital.

When my mom, my three sisters, and I arrived at the hospital, we were ushered into the family waiting room to wait for Dad's doctor to give us an update on his condition. About three hours later, the doctor came to speak with the Robinson family. We all went into the conference room where he introduced himself and asked who each of us were in relationship to my father. He said Dad aspirated as he was choking on a piece of pork chop. He had a nasal cannula in his nose because his breathing was labored, and he was not getting enough oxygen. The doctor said he would stay in ICU so they could watch him closely.

The next three days, Dad's oxygen level was erratic, and we were told he would have a tracheotomy. We met with one of the heads of the department who said our father was near death; if he survived, he would have to be placed on life support because his muscle strength was weak due to his Parkinson's disease. He would never be able to eat, and would most likely be braindead.

The department head wanted to know who would be responsible for making the decision to let Dad go to glory. We looked at one another and Deborah said, "Our mother would have to make that call because he is her husband first and our dad second." All of us nodded in agreement. My mother said God would have to make that decision. We all voiced our opinion. I said I don't believe any of the diagnoses, and my sisters agreed. We went back to the family waiting room to get some rest. Mom stayed in the room with our father.

After weeks in ICU, my father was transported to Select Care, which is a long-term facility for critical patients. I went to see my father daily. One morning, his pulmonary doctor was in his room. I introduced myself telling him I was Mr. Robinson's eldest daughter. I asked how long it would be before my dad could eat food. He said six months.

"That's a long time not to be able to eat," I said.

"Well, maybe three months," he replied.

"That's still a long time to not be able to eat."

"You know he died," the doctor lashed out.

I answered, "But just like Lazarus, he was raised from the dead."

He looked up thinking and said, "Oh yes, just like the phoenix bird."

I did not agree.

I looked at this handsome, immaculately dressed doctor and thought to myself, he doesn't even know who Lazarus is. Lazarus's name means God has helped, and he was comparing him to Greek mythology. Wow!

I went to see my father a few days after my encounter with the runway model doctor. I was just about to enter my father's room when I heard code blue over the intercom. Two nurses brushed pass me entering the room. Another nurse told me to go back into the waiting room and someone would come talk to me.

I sat anxiously waiting. As another nurse passed by, I asked her what code blue was. She said they were just readjusting my father's tracheotomy, and I would be able to see him soon. I went in and sat with Dad about an hour and left not wanting to tire him out.

Later that night I learned my sister Demetrice went by to see Dad, and the nurse explained to her our father's trach worked its way out for the third time that day. The nurse said every time they put it in, it pushed its way back out. The nurse called Dr. Mullins, wanting to know what to do next. She said the doctor loudly said feed him! I knew just like Yeshua loved Lazarus, He went before His Father on my dad's behalf. He allowed my dad to get his heart's desire which was to go home. My dad left the Select Care unit and went to a nursing care facility not far from home.

About four weeks later, our family rejoiced when our father who was given no chance, returned home eating and talking with no brain challenges whatsoever. What a mighty God we serve!

Meditative Scriptures

Then said Yeshua to them plainly, Lazarus is dead.
And I'm glad for your sakes that I was not there, to
the intent you may believe; nevertheless, let us go
unto him.
John 11:14

Then they took away the stone from the place
where the dead was laid. And Yeshua lifted up His
eyes and said, ABBA, I thank thee that
thou has heard me and I knew that
thou hearest me always, but because of the people
which stand by, I said it that they may believe that
thou has sent me. And when He thus had spoken,
He cried with a loud voice, Lazarus come forth.
And he that was dead came forth, bound hand and
foot with grave clothes: and his face was bound
with a napkin; Yeshua said unto them loose
him and let him go.
John 11:41-44

Reflective Thoughts

....

....

....

....

....

....

....

....

....

....

Miracles Happen Daily

· ·

· ·

· ·

· ·

· ·

· ·

· ·

· ·

· ·

· ·

· ·

· ·

· ·

· ·

About the Author

Author Antoinette Robinson Dunham is a wife, mother, grandmother, retired cosmetologist and missionary. She has spent most of her life helping and caring for people. She believes that serving is the call for every follower of Yeshua. By sharing these true-life miracles, she hopes to encourage those who have gone through loss of family or friends, and obstacles that life's journey presents. She currently resides in Savannah, Georgia, a historical and beautiful city on the East Coast.

Miracles Happen Daily